THE OFFICIAL
EVERTON
FOOTBALL CLUB ANNUAL 2015

Written by Darren Griffiths and Hamish Dufton
Designed by Cavan Convery

A Grange Publication

© 2014. Published by Grange Communications Ltd., Edinburgh, under licence from Everton Football Club. Printed in the EU.

Photographs © Everton Football Club.

ISBN: 978-1-908925-66-4

£7.99

CONTENTS

ROBERTO MARTÍNEZ

In this day and age, where there's football, there's the press!

Roberto Martínez and his players are frequently fulfilling media duties down at Finch Farm or at games and are always posed a variety of questions. That means they ended up talking about all sorts of things!

Below are some of the things from the 2013/14 season that our Spanish boss said in interviews...

THE BOSS ON...

Doing the double over Man United:

"It was more than pleasing. It was an outstanding result and the first time we have done the double over Manchester United since 1969. I couldn't be prouder.

"We knew we were facing a very good side. Their away record is excellent but we were focused and controlled the game and were electrifying on the counter-attack.

"We worked hard to keep a clean sheet. That is difficult to do when you take a two-goal lead, especially against Manchester United. It speaks volumes of the togetherness and focus of this team."

THE BOSS ON...

Beating Arsenal 3-0 at Goodison:

"In terms of satisfaction that you can get as a manager, that's as good as it gets. I thought the performance from the first minute to the last was very strong in every department of the game.

"We had to be perfect in the way we wanted to defend, the way we wanted to use the counter-attack, the way we wanted to be a threat in the final third and the way we wanted to keep possession.

"The players were phenomenal – their awareness, work rate and discipline made it as good a performance as you can get from that point of view."

THE BOSS ON...

Seamus Coleman's award-winning season:

"He's got that good arrogance – a footballing arrogance. You can't teach that. Seamus has had that for a long, long time, it's just being able to express himself like that on top of all his duties and the responsible things he has to do for the team.

"I haven't done anything to coax that out of him. He knows his potential. He plays in a demanding position which needs you to be so good in many areas.

"Seamus is a good example of a footballer with an incredible attitude and appetite for the game. He grows month by month. He's one of the best full-backs in world football."

The gaffer is bound to provide some more great quotes this season so we've left you some boxes to fill in any you really like! Listen to what he says on Sky Sports, Match of the Day and on the radio and make a note of your favourite quotes!

THE BOSS ON...

Gareth Barry's debut v Chelsea:

"It was a masterclass. It's very difficult when you're not playing to keep working hard and keep your fitness up. He is full of knowledge. He is one of those profiles that you don't get in the English game.

"He's the perfect influence for Ross Barkley and James McCarthy, but I thought his partnership with Leon Osman was magnificent. Remember that Chelsea are at their best in that area. They're clever and use the space really well. They have really good individuals in one-on-one situations. I thought Gareth Barry was essential when it came to keeping a clean sheet."

Making his Blues debut against QPR

THE ROSS BARKLEY STORY
from Wavertree to the World Cup

Ever since Ross Barkley could walk, he was kicking a ball. The young Evertonian was always out and about, pretending the streets and parks of Wavertree were actually Goodison Park or Wembley, and dreaming of one day pulling on the royal blue jersey.

Playing for his local team at the weekends, his incredible talent was soon spotted by Everton scouts – his dreams were about to come true!

Ross joined Everton aged 11 and started playing for the Blues younger age groups. However he was soon playing for the age group above his own. Before long, at 14, he was playing for the Under-16s.

Barkley's impressive form for Everton saw him called up by England to make his Under-16s debut and he went on to help them win the prestigious Montaigu Tournament in France in 2009.

A year later, Barkley was called up to represent England's Under-17s alongside fellow Blue Luke Garbutt for the European Championships. The young Lions were drawn in a group with Turkey, Czech Republic and Greece.

Ross scored the first goal in a 3-1 win over the Czechs, then the winner against Greece before

helping England defeat the Turks as well!

The Three Lions then beat France to reach the final, where they faced Spain. Despite former Everton winger Gerard Deulofeu opening the scoring, England fought back to lift the trophy.

Celebrating his Goal of the Season against Manchester City

Barkley's meteoric rise continued as he was named to the first team bench on occasion throughout the early part of the 2010/11 season but his progress would be stopped in its tracks by a serious injury.

By this time he was playing for England's Under-19s and during a European Championships qualifier against Belgium he collided with Liverpool's Andre Wisdom and broke his leg in three places.

However, it was merely a speed bump on the road to the first team. Barkley recovered in time to be involved with the first team for pre-season ahead of the 2011/12 campaign. His hard work was then rewarded by being named in the starting XI for the season opener against QPR, being named Man of the Match after a fantastic display.

He made a further eight appearances that season and signed a new long-term contract.

Ross played far more football in 2012/13. He took in a couple of loan spells at Sheffield Wednesday and Leeds United before returning to make 11 appearances for the Blues.

At the end of the season he was named in the England Under-20 squad for the Under-20s World Cup, and upon his return from that tournament, scored his first goal for the Under-21 side in a 6-0 win over Scotland.

In August 2013, he then graduated to the senior squad and made his debut in a World Cup qualifier against Moldova.

However it wasn't until the arrival of Roberto Martínez that the Ross Barkley story really reaches its climax.

The Spaniard immediately added Ross to his squad and started him against Norwich in his first game in charge. And Barkley scored a peach of goal to put Everton ahead at Carrow Road!

It was the first of seven goals Ross would score throughout the 2013/14 season. Some of them were simply amazing – who remembers his mazy dribble at Newcastle United or the incredible free-kick at Swansea or THAT goal against Manchester City?!

That strike earned him the Goal of the Season award at the annual Club Awards evening, where he also scooped the Young Player of the Year prize.

His exciting play and great form saw Ross called up for the England squad for the World Cup in Brazil and he featured in all three group matches against Italy, Uruguay and Costa Rica.

While that tournament wasn't the best for England, the emergence of Ross Barkley as a future Three Lions mainstay was certainly a big plus point for us Everton fans.

But what's more important? We can watch his story continue every week at Goodison!

In pre-season action against Werder Bremen ahead of the 2011/12 season

STRANGE BUT TRUE...!

Here are some weird and wonderful facts about your favourite football club that will amaze you and your friends...

In 2002/03 Everton became the first club to play 100 seasons in the English top-division. We have played more top-flight games than any other team.

Only five goalkeepers have ever scored goals in the Premier League and two of those goals have been scored at the Gwladys Street End at Goodison Park! Peter Schmeichel did so for Aston Villa against us in 2001 and Tim Howard scored against Bolton in 2012, although that was wind assisted!!!

James Vaughan celebrates becoming Everton's youngest ever scorer in 2005

Tim Howard celebrates his amazing goal against Bolton in 2012

Despite more than 60 Everton players appearing for England, it was not until the friendly against Honduras just before the 2014 World Cup that one of them wore the captain's armband for the very first time – Phil Jagielka becoming the main man.

Goodison Park is the only league ground in the country to have a church attached – St Luke's on the corner of Gwladys Street.

Duncan Ferguson has scored a record 60 Premier League goals for Everton – not surprisingly more than half were headers!

Football nets were invented after a famous Liverpool engineer called John Brodie saw a dispute in an Everton home game in 1889. The Everton players argued that the ball had gone between the posts but the referee said it had gone wide!! Brodie's nets were used in goals for the first time two years later.

At the start of the 2014/15 season, Everton's James Vaughan was still the youngest ever Premier League goalscorer. The Academy graduate scored against Crystal Palace aged just 16 years 270 days in 2005.

Phil Jagielka became Everton's first ever England captain in 2014

Two players have scored a club record 18 goals for their country whilst with the Toffees – the great Dixie Dean for England and modern-day legend Tim Cahill, who did so for Australia.

Only one Everton game at Goodison has been suspended due to floodlight failure – against Manchester United in 1975.

Tim Cahill scored 18 international goals whilst an Everton player

Goodison Park is the only ground in the UK with a church attached to it!

Many years ago clubs used to play on Christmas Day in every season, but this stopped a long time ago. Our last game on 25th December was against Bolton in 1957.

Legendary keeper Neville Southall's Everton appearance record may never be beaten the great man playing 751 times from 1981-1997.

Goodison can fit about 39,000 spectators inside the ground these days, but it once held twice that number when 78,000 watched a derby game against Liverpool in 1948. Thankfully most were standing!!

In 2014, Leon Osman overtook David Unsworth as the Everton player with the most Premier League appearances.

During our game at West Brom in the 1970s a Jack Russell dog got onto the pitch and took the ball off Ken McNaught, the Everton centre-half! The ball ran loose and into the path of Baggies' striker David Cross who scored easily. The referee allowed the goal to stand and the dog claimed an assist!!

Neville Southall has played more times for Everton than anyone else

Everton's Premier League record appearance maker is Leon Osman

Blues' legend Kevin Ratcliffe is the last Everton outfielder to don the goalkeeper's gloves during a game, doing so at Chelsea in 1985 when Neville Southall was sent-off (there was no goalkeeping substitutes in those days). Ratcliffe kept a clean sheet in his 31 minutes in goal as well!

11

PLAYER PROFILES

PART 1

See what the Everton players think of each other!

Each member of the squad has been analysed by one of his team-mates, the boss or an ex-player!

Have a read of them and see if you agree... we've left space for you to add your own profile.

ANTOLÍN ALCARAZ

ROBERTO MARTÍNEZ SAYS: *"Antolín is good in the air, strong and powerful in one versus one situations and defensively he can read the game really, really well. On the ball, he is a modern footballer who plays from the back and can start the play. He is a complete centre-half and fits very well with the other centre-halves we have at the club."*

LEIGHTON BAINES

SYLVAIN DISTIN SAYS: *"He is definitely one of the best I have played with. He is a top player. He can pass, he can tackle, he can cross, score free-kicks – he is an amazing player. Bainesy is part of the group who stay behind after training and do extra work in the gym. He is looking after himself and you can see the results on the pitch."*

ROSS BARKLEY

PHIL JAGIELKA SAYS: *"Ross is a fantastic player and he's obviously very frustrating to play against because he's got a tremendous amount of ability. He's grown not only as a player but as a person over these last 12 months and you can see the confidence, playing pretty much week in and week out, has given him. That has helped his game develop."*

SEAMUS COLEMAN

TIM HOWARD SAYS: *"He's a hard worker and a humble guy. He works really hard and he is everything you could ask for in a teammate and professional. Seamus is brilliant in one-on-ones, he has got pace and stamina – he will go from defending at the back post and edging someone out to sprinting up the pitch and supporting the winger and getting in the box for a cross or shot."*

SYLVAIN DISTIN

ROBERTO MARTÍNEZ SAYS: *"I'm proud to have a player like Sylvain representing Everton because he has got incredible standards. He has been an incredible performer and has stepped up and gone to a different level. He has always been paramount in our defensive duties but now he is very important in our style of play and the distribution that he brings to the team. Sylvain looks after himself – he is always the last man out at Finch Farm and he could play for a long, long time."*

SHANE DUFFY

SYLVAIN DISTIN SAYS: *"What I am sure about is that I've seen enough of Shane Duffy to feel comfortable with him being able to play in the Premier League and I'm pretty sure he already proved it a few seasons ago when, because of injuries, he had to play and he did a great job."*

DARRON GIBSON

SEAMUS COLEMAN SAYS: *"Darron has been brilliant since he came to Everton. I know he's been injured at times but ask any Everton fan since he's come from Manchester United and they'll tell you he's been brilliant. His range of passing is great and he is a real asset. He is a good ball player and he can get about the pitch as well."*

END OF SEASON AWARDS

Back in the summer, Everton Football Club celebrated the 2013/14 campaign with an End of Season Awards night at St. George's Hall in Liverpool.

It was here that the prestigious Player of the Season was named, along with a number of other awards.

BT Sports' presenter Jake Humphrey fulfilled MC duties as the night kicked off with the naming of the next 'Everton Giant'. The late, great Bobby Collins took the honours with his son Robert taking to the stage to collect the award.

Next up was Young Player of the Year, and the winner was...Ross Barkley!

Continuing of the theme of young Evertonians, fellow youth set-up graduate Ryan Ledson was named Academy Player of the Season. Keep an eye out for him in the coming seasons!

Then it was on to the Ladies Player of the Year which was won by striker Nikita Parris, who collected her award from Tony Hibbert and Leon Osman.

Next up on stage was Tyias Browning, who collected the Under-21s Player of the Year prize.

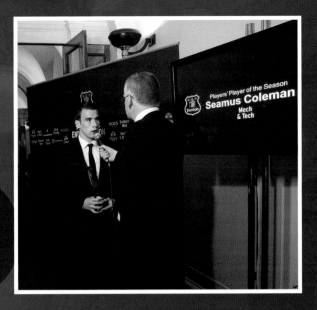

Well, there was only one obvious winner – Seamus Coleman! "When I arrived here in 2009, I couldn't have imagined I'd be stood here with these awards in my hands," he said after picking up the prize. "There must have been a lot of contenders for both of these awards this season and that says a lot about this team."

There was just time then for the Chairman Bill Kenwright to hand Roberto Martínez his Blueblood award for an outstanding debut season at the Goodison Park helm, before choruses of 'Allez Allez Allez Oooh' rang out around St. George's Hall!

Everton's most successful ever chairman Sir Philip Carter was then honoured for his unwavering loyalty to the football club with the Howard Kendall Award, and then Seamus Coleman scooped one of the most popular awards in the game – the Players' Player of the Year award, voted for by the players at Finch Farm.

Ross was then back on stage to pick up his second award of the night as he won the Goal of the Season award for his awesome strike against Manchester City.

Now it was the time everyone had been waiting for – who would walk away with the coveted Player of the Year award?

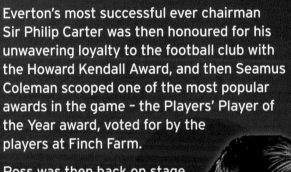

INTERNATIONAL BLUES

Everton have always had international players within their ranks - from all corners of the globe!

From Costa Rica to Australia to Israel to China, the Blues have had players represent their countries across the world. Even now we have no less than 18 players ready and waiting for an international call-up.

We all know who Seamus Coleman, Ross Barkley, Kevin Mirallas and Tim Howard play for but what about these former Blues?

Can you match the head to the body and piece together which old Everton player is representing which country?

Answers on page 60-61.

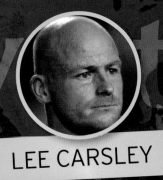

LEE CARSLEY

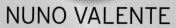

NUNO VALENTE

LOUIS SAHA

AUSTRALIA

DENMARK

HOLLAND

ECUADOR

RUSSIA

THOMAS GRAVESEN

TIM CAHILL

LANDON DONOVAN

SEGUNDO CASTILLO

NIGERIA

PORTUGAL

USA

FRANCE

IRELAND

JOSEPH YOBO

DINIYAR BILYALETDINOV

JOHN HEITINGA

1878

1906 FA CUP FINAL

EVERTON
HONOURS BOARD

FIRST DIVISION CHAMPIONS	FIRST DIVISION RUNNERS-UP	FA CUP WINNERS	EUROPEAN CUP WINNERS' CUP WINNERS
1890/91	1889/90	1906	1985
1914/15	1894/95	1933	
1927/28	1901/02	1966	
1931/32	1904/05	1984	
1938/39	1908/09	1995	
1962/63	1911/12		
1969/70	1985/86		
1984/85			
1986/87			

1933 FA CUP

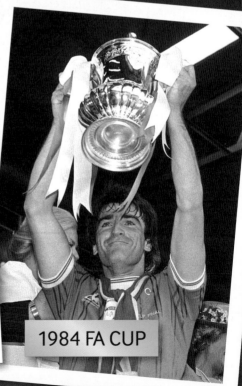

1984 FA CUP

1963 CHAMPIONS

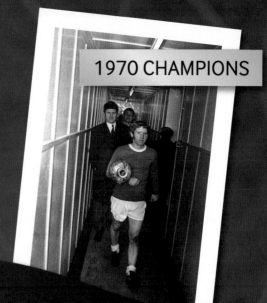

1970 CHAMPIONS

EVERTON
HONOURS BOARD

FA CHARITY SHIELD	FA CUP RUNNERS-UP	FOOTBALLER OF THE YEAR	NATIONAL FA PREMIER ACADEMY LEAGUE CHAMPIONS
1928	1893	1984/85 NEVILLE SOUTHALL	2010/11
1932	1897		2013/14
1963	1907	1985/86 GARY LINEKER	
1970	1968		
1984	1985	**PFA PLAYER OF THE YEAR**	**FA YOUTH CUP**
1985	1986	1984/85 PETER REID	1965
1986 (Shared)	1989		1984
1987	2009	1985/86 GARY LINEKER	1998
1995			

1995 FA CUP

1966 FA CUP

WORDSEARCH

Find the names in the grid. Words can go horizontally, vertically and diagonally in all eight directions. Answers on page 60-61.

Alcaraz
Atsu
Baines

Barkley
Barry
Besic
Coleman

Gibson
Howard
Jagielka

W	Q	X	B	G	O	D	E	I	V	O	B	N
Y	M	I	R	A	L	L	A	S	T	K	A	K
W	P	I	E	N	A	A	R	R	N	T	R	C
H	T	I	M	S	I	A	N	S	F	C	R	F
C	T	C	J	A	G	I	E	L	K	A	Y	M
D	N	G	O	D	U	N	G	M	T	E	N	C
R	Z	O	M	L	I	K	C	L	Y	N	K	C
A	A	C	S	A	E	G	A	E	N	O	V	A
W	R	B	B	B	E	M	L	K	N	K	T	R
O	A	D	E	A	I	K	A	A	U	S	R	T
H	C	P	D	S	R	G	M	N	U	L	R	H
C	L	Y	T	A	I	S	E	N	O	T	S	Y
F	A	T	B	F	O	C	M	N	Y	L	V	Q

Kone
Lukaku

McCarthy
McGeady
Mirallas

Naismith
Osman
Oviedo

Pienaar
Stones

JUNIOR FANS' FORUM

The Everton Junior Fans' Forum was launched in August 2013 to give junior Blues the chance to share their views and get involved in key decisions that are likely to affect them.

The group of 10 youngsters are all aged between 11-17 and meet with Club officials every half term to discuss a variety of topics. (The members are changed every season to give more junior blues a chance to engage with the Club.)

Members completed an online application form to be a part of the Forum and our Fan Ambassador Graeme Sharp selected all successful applicants.

The Junior Fans' Forum has made a real impact since being created in 2013. Within their first 12 months they had many successes, with one of their biggest arriving in January 2014 when they helped the Club to bring Junior Fans' Day to life at the home fixture against Norwich City.

It was the inspiration of the Junior Fans' Forum to bring a mini-match day team to

Goodison Park that day to give them a unique behind-the-scenes insight... so we had a mini-receptionist, mini-match officials, mini-security, mini-ground staff, mini-Everton TV reporters and even a mini-Roberto!

The young fans also gave their input into the crest consultation, interviewed the Club's deputy Chief Executive Officer, Denise Barrett-Baxendale, and put forward their ideas for the brand new evertonfc.com that was launched in August 2014.

They also helped to arrange the Junior Blues Sports Day at Finch Farm, took up a mystery shopping experience at the Club stores and got the chance to put their questions to manager Roberto Martínez in an exclusive interview.

In addition to giving young fans the opportunity to get involved, the Junior Fans' Forum provides a valuable opportunity for the Club to gain feedback from an ever-increasing section of the fan base.

As part of its continued commitment to fan engagement, the Club is in constant dialogue with supporters and the junior initiative is an extension of the adult Fans' Forum, who meets regularly with Club officials.

Keep an eye on evertonfc.com at the end of the season to see how YOU can get involved...

TONY BELLEW TRAINING TIPS

TIP 1

STAY HYDRATED!

The minute that you become dehydrated your performance can reduce and the work you do might not be as effective. Things like electrolyte drinks can help keep you hydrated and ensure your performance levels are maintained at a high standard.

TIP 2

WEAR THE RIGHT GEAR!

Depending on the temperature or the weather, wearing the right clothing is important. If it's cold you need to keep your body warm. I wear Nike Pro stuff myself but Umbro have their range as well. This is important to help avoid injuries but it also helps with movements and not hyper-extending your arms for example. In boxing there are so many different things to look out for, but whatever you are doing you have got to be careful.

TIP 3

USE THE BEST EQUIPMENT!

As a boxer, I use a lot of equipment and I have to trust it to do what it's supposed to do. I have to tape my hands up just right or I could injure myself and my gloves have to be of good quality. Good equipment is vital as a precaution against things like injuries. Be very selective in what you use and how you use it.

TIP 4

STICK TO YOUR SCHEDULE!

It can be tough but if you have planned to go for a run – stick to your schedule. On top of that, make sure you stick to your targets. That way you will give yourself the best chance of achieving the best results you possibly can. Like the tip above – when running, footwear is all important. I wear Asics just because they feel the best for me but there are various different brands now so pick the one that suits you.

TIP 5 — WATCH YOUR DIET!

Your diet can be really important when doing exercise. Without the right kind of fuel in the body, the engine ain't going to work — it's as simple as that. It's not necessarily about eating lots of healthy food. You need to eat the correct amount of a balanced diet at the right times. You need the right amount of protein as much as you need the right amount of vegetables or carbohydrates. If you do that you will get the best out of the food you eat and subsequently the best out of your body.

TIP 6 — THE OTHER GUY IS WORKING HARDER THAN YOU!

Regardless of what sport or exercise you do — hard work is so important. What keeps me going and gets me out of bed in the morning to go running is the knowledge that my opponent is doing everything he can to be in best possible shape. It's that competition that can drive you to keep working as hard as you can. Can you do more than the other guy is doing? It can be applied to things like football — if you are a defender then you want to be better and fitter than your opposition's striker.

TIP 7 — ALWAYS LISTEN TO YOUR COACHES!

Your coach is vital. If you are lucky enough to have a really top coach, like I've had throughout my career, then listen to them. A coach will see many things that you will not. It's very different looking at a sporting event - be it a football match, a boxing bout or whatever — from a distance compared to looking at it from being in it. A coach will see the things that an athlete will never see — what's happening, how it's getting done, mistakes the other guy is making and how to exploit them. As the athlete, there is usually so much going on in your mind so you need that advice and that strategy to succeed.

TIP 8 — YOU CAN DO TOO MUCH!

In tip six, I said that you want to do more than your opponent but be careful — it can be a catch-22. Too much exercise and training can be harmful. You need the right people around you to let you know when enough is enough. And you need to trust them!

TIP 9 — ENJOY YOUR SUCCESS!

When you are playing for fun — enjoy yourself. Once you reach that elite level, it becomes work and you don't enjoy it no more! What I would say though is enjoy your victories. Your next one could be your very last. You have got to be positive, be strong-minded and savour the moment, especially your successes!

NEW KIT PHOTO-SHOOT

Whenever a Premier League match is screened 'live' on television you will see that when the team line-ups are announced the players are shown walking towards the screen.

This is all filmed at the training ground and when the cameras rock up to Finch Farm it's a very busy day!

Each player who is likely to feature in the first team squad throughout the course of the season needs to be filmed. And not just in the home kit either – they need to do it in the away strip and the third kit.

So Finch Farm resembles a film studio for a day!

At the start of the 2014/15 season Sky Sports, BT Sport and EvertonTV all set up what is called their 'green screen' in the huge indoor gym at the training ground.

The crews arrived at 7am and rigged up huge green cloths (green is the easiest colour to super-impose a background onto) and from 9am the players started to troop through.

Some did it before training, some did it after, some did their filming in one take and others took a while!

It's a fun day... but it's also a bit chaotic at times... especially when there's a queue of players waiting to be filmed.

THE DUNCAN FERGUSON STORY

Duncan Ferguson was born in the Scottish city of Stirling. He was always tall for his age and showed good prowess as a youngster, playing regularly for local teams as well as his school side. His first professional team was Dundee United in the Scottish Premier League and he made his debut in November 1990.

The young Ferguson proved himself to be a handful for more experienced defenders and he earned himself a call-up to the Scotland Under-21s squad.

His name began to be linked with bigger and better teams and it was to Glasgow Rangers that the 22-year old centre-forward moved in 1993.

Unfortunately, it turned out to be an ill-fated move for Ferguson. He never truly settled and an incident during a match against Raith Rovers at Ibrox eventually led to his imprisonment 18 months later.

It was becoming increasingly clear that a move away from Glasgow would be in the best interests

of the player and the Everton manager Mike Walker brought him to Merseyside for a loan spell along with Ferguson's Rangers team-mate Ian Durrant in October 1994.

The big striker had found his spiritual home! The Evertonians loved his aggressive, cavalier style and he in turn felt the same way about the Goodison supporters.

Mike Walker was sacked in November 1994 and a former Everton centre-forward Joe Royle took over as manager. Royle got the very best out of Ferguson and after the big fellow scored his first goal in a 2-0 Merseyside derby win against Liverpool at Goodison the clamour to sign him permanently reached fever pitch!

A deal was duly agreed with Rangers and Ferguson set about making himself an Everton legend.

He scored the winner against Manchester United at Goodison when he out-jumped Peter Schmeichel to head the only goal of the game in February 1995 and ended his first season at Everton with an FA Cup winner's medal.

So the big man is back where he belongs! He may be in the dug-out rather than on the pitch but the fans still chant his name at every game and for a man who has royal blue blood running through his veins, that's as good as it gets!

The mid and late-90s weren't very successful for Everton but Ferguson was still a hero and the supporters were shocked and upset by his surprise departure to Newcastle United in October 1998.

Ruud Gullit was the Newcastle manager at the time and his idea was to form a partnership between Ferguson and Alan Shearer.

Sadly for the Scot his time at St James' Park was blighted by injuries and although the 'Toon Army' saw glimpses of his ability, they never really saw the best of him.

In August 2000 every Evertonian's dream came true when Walter Smith re-signed Ferguson from Newcastle and in typical fashion the big man scored twice on his second debut against Charlton Athletic.

Ferguson later became the captain of Everton Football Club and in May 2006 he played his last ever game for the club against West Bromwich Albion and scored his last goal with virtually his last kick!

He then went into retirement abroad and was very rarely seen until he returned to Everton in 2012 as an Academy coach. He assisted Kevin Sheedy with the Under-18s and such was his prowess and enthusiasm that last season Roberto Martínez invited him to join the first-team staff.

PLAYER PROFILES PART 2

TONY HIBBERT

ROBERTO MARTÍNEZ SAYS: *"In my eyes Tony has got a lot to offer at Everton. I value his contribution at the club and his experience. In terms of his day-to-day work, he's been magnificent and I'd go as far as saying he's been paramount in keeping really strong standards in our training sessions, in making sure that the group was ready, helping out the youngsters and every time he has played he has performed well."*

TIM HOWARD

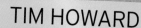

ROBERTO MARTÍNEZ SAYS: *"Tim has been faultless. He is a special footballer and human being at Everton because he represents everything I want from a player. He has incredible professionalism, a great vision and he influences people around him. He is someone as good as you will see in this league. He has played an incredible role in how we want to start our play and continues to improve and make himself better."*

PHIL JAGIELKA

ROBERTO MARTÍNEZ SAYS: *"I've been a big admirer of Phil Jagielka and his example is representative of the standards of our football club on a daily basis. He has embraced the role as captain and has been a perfect fit for a role that is traditionally a great honour at the football club. He's always had a real presence in the dressing room and had plenty of wise words of advice for the young players in the squad. He's our club captain and we need him out on the pitch."*

AROUNA KONÉ

ROBERTO MARTÍNEZ SAYS: *"He's got everything that an Evertonian would expect of a striker - the work ethic, the technical ability to score goals – they are always essential in a striker. But probably the biggest strength that Arouna has is that calmness in front of goal, that composure to be a real reference for the team. He is someone who copes with the physicality of the game and brings a really strong back-to-goal play in the forward position."*

_____

_____

JAMES MCCARTHY

SEAMUS COLEMAN SAYS: *"I feel comfortable in the right-back position now and thankfully I have got James in midfield who, when I do bomb on, covers me brilliantly. Without him I probably wouldn't have been doing as many forward runs in games as I have done because I can trust him to cover me. He has been brilliant."*

_____

_____

AIDEN MCGEADY

Former Everton and Ireland midfielder LEE CARSLEY SAYS: *"I played with Aiden for Ireland. Our international careers overlapped by about four years. He's a good player, an out-and-out winger and is very tricky. He is a terrific addition to the squad. Aiden is someone who has a lot of talent, a lot of skill and is very different to anyone we have in the squad."*

_____

_____

KEVIN MIRALLAS

ROBERTO MARTÍNEZ SAYS: *"Kevin is desperate to set standards week in, week out. And that, for a striker or attacking player, is very rare and that is why I had no problems of playing him in different positions and moving him around because I think he has that maturity. It is that mentality of knowing how important he is for our football club and the squad. He brings that star quality."*

_____

_____

29

EVERTON
IN THE
COMMUNITY

Everton Football Club has its own charity called Everton in the Community that helps thousands of people from all over Merseyside every year.

For over 26 years, the charity has been helping people, young and old, from many different backgrounds in lots of ways including health, education and helping people into employment.

Everton in the Community works with children and adults to teach them about the benefits of eating healthily and doing regular exercise and also helps people find new jobs and gain qualifications.

A few nights a week, the charity runs a programme called Kicks all over Liverpool which gives young people a safe place to play sports and keep them off the streets and out of trouble and the Safe Hands programme helps young adults who have been in trouble with the police get their lives back on track.

Many of the programmes that Everton in the Community deliver are funded by the Premier League and one of these is called Premier League 4 Sport and gives school children the opportunity to try sports that were popular in the London 2012 Olympics including judo, table tennis and hockey.

The charity doesn't just help children and teenagers. It helps ex-soldiers and young men who struggle with mental health problems and one of its newest programmes, Pass on the Memories, helps older people who are experiencing memory loss.

The charity has the biggest and most successful disability football programme in the

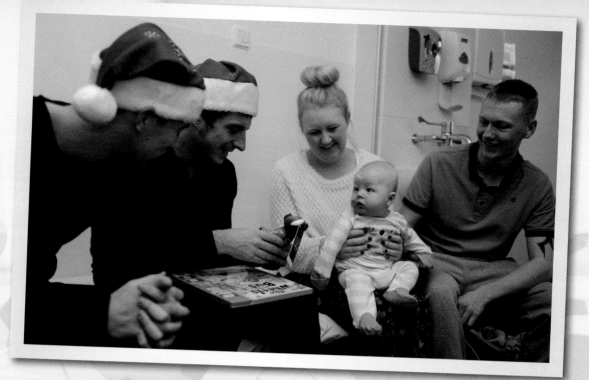

world and has 26 different teams for all ages and abilities.

Everton even has its own Free School which is open to young people aged 14-19 and offers alternative educational opportunities.

Throughout the season, Roberto Martínez and his players visit lots of Everton in the Community programmes to find out more about the great work they do and to meet the people that the charity helps. Sometimes the players get involved with classroom or sports sessions with children and other times they spend time playing bingo with old people who are struggling with memory loss.

At Christmas time, the full team visit sick children at Alder Hey Children's Hospital and deliver presents to help put smiles on the faces of them and their families.

The work that Everton in the Community does is recognised by people all over the year and last year the charity got 19 awards for its brilliant ground-breaking work including one from the Prime Minister David Cameron.

The charity also fundraises throughout the year to raise money to help them continue their impressive work and there are lots of different ways that fans can get involved to help. Some fans have done a skydive, some do marathon runs and local schools have held sponsored silences and cake stalls to help the charity of their favourite club.

BRAZIL 2014

At the end of last season, not one Evertonian wanted to take a break from the glorious football on show at Goodison Park. Thankfully we had a World Cup to help us cope!

And what a tournament it was. From the surprise early exits of Spain and Italy to the Hollywood story of Costa Rica and the heroics of the USA, the 20th World Cup was a cracker.

Phil Jagielka heads the ball off the line against Italy

Tim Howard prepares to swap shirts with Romelu Lukaku after their last-16 clash

Ok so England's tournament didn't exactly go according to plan but for us Evertonians it was great to see Leighton Baines, Phil Jagielka and Ross Barkley playing against some of the greatest players in the game.

Then we had Kevin Mirallas – and Romelu Lukaku! – doing their thing for Belgium. Super Kev made two appearances as the Red Devils cruised through Group H, seeing off Algeria, Russia and South Korea.

WHO DID I PLAY FOR?

For which countries did these 10 Premier League players appear during the 2014 World Cup?

1. Wilfried Bony (Swansea City)
2. Santi Cazorla (Arsenal)
3. Edin Džeko (Man City)
4. Pablo Zabaleta (Man City)
5. Antonio Valencia (Man United)
6. Javier Hernández (Man United)
7. Tim Krul (Newcastle United)
8. Gastón Ramírez (Southampton)
9. Geoff Cameron (Stoke City)
10. Paulinho (Tottenham Hotspur)

Answers on page 60-61.

Ross Barkley has a shot for England against Italy

exertions in the previous round caught up with them and they lost 1-0, meaning all our Everton boys were heading home.

But as you can see from the pictures, they certainly had made their mark on a fantastic tournament!

Romelu Lukaku in action against Russia

The Belgians then drew Tim Howard's USA in the round of 16.

T-How had been ever-present as the USMNT safely negotiated the supposed 'Group of Death', earning a victory over Ghana, then coming within a whisker of defeating Portugal (only to concede a last minute equaliser in a 2-2 draw) before finally going through as runners-up behind Germany.

And, in one of the games of the tournament, both Howard and Mirallas featured in a pulsating 2-1 win for Belgium.

Mirallas and his countrymen then faced eventual finalists Argentina, but their

WORLD CUP QUIZ

1. What was the score when Germany defeated Brazil in the semi-final?

2. England only scored two goals – which two players got them?

3. Which former Everton player played for Nigeria?

4. Who ended the tournament as the top goalscorer?

5. Name the four Chelsea players who played for Brazil?

6. By what scoreline did Holland beat Spain in the group stage?

7. In Group B, how many points did Tim Cahill's Australia get – two, one or none?

8. How many times have Germany and Argentina met in the final – once, twice or three times?

9. What was Ross Barkley's England squad number?

10. Where will the 2018 World Cup be held?

Kevin Mirallas is denied by Tim Howard when Belgium played USA

Answers on page 60-61.

SPOT the DIFFERENCE

Can you spot six differences between the pictures below?
Answers on page 60-61.

JUNIOR QUIZ

Here are 15 questions to test your knowledge of Everton.
See how many you get right and see if you can beat the
grown-up who tackles their special quiz on Page 59!

1. For what country does Antolín Alcaraz play?

2. Which Everton player was sent-off in the 2010 World Cup final?

3. Apart from Everton and Wigan, which other team has Roberto Martínez managed?

4. Which team knocked Everton out of last season's Capital One Cup?

5. Who were Everton's main sponsors before Chang?

6. From which team did Everton sign Phil Jagielka?

7. At Goodison Park, which stand is directly opposite the Main Stand?

8. Who was the last player to score for Everton at Wembley?

9. Ross Barkley was on loan at which two Championship teams in 2012/13?

10. Who did Everton play on the last day of last season and what was the score?

11. Who scored the Everton goals in last season's 3-3 draw with Liverpool?

12. And who netted the three in the 3-0 win at Newcastle United?

13. Who had the squad number 26 last season?

14. Name the other three teams in England's 2014 World Cup group in Brazil?

15. Of the following defenders to have played for Everton last season, who was the only one to score a goal? Distin, Heitinga, Jagielka, Stones?

Answers on page 60-61.

STAY IN THE KNOW!

Enjoying this year's Official Everton Annual? Of course you are!

But did you know there are now loads of ways to keep up-to-date with the goings on at Goodison Park!

Here's how you can impress all your classmates by staying clued up on the Blues...

evertonfc.com

evertonfc.com has a new look and is now bigger and better than ever before!

Designed to look super impressive on your computer screen, tablet and phone, the Club's official website brings you all the big headlines coming out of Goodison Park, as well as the very best coverage of matchdays – from Roberto's pre-game press conference at Finch Farm, right through to post-match interviews with your Blues heroes just moments after the full-time whistle.

With a new interactive history section, more match stats and improved player profiles, the all-new evertonfc.com is not to be missed!

evertontv

Everyone loves videos – and evertontv brings you more footage of the Blues than anyone else.

With evertontv, you can go behind-the-scenes at Finch Farm, watch interviews with manager Roberto Martínez and all your favourite players, get highlights of every single first-team and Under-21s game, learn more about the Club's official charity Everton in the Community and, guess what? It's absolutely free!

To see everything evertontv has to offer, simply log on to **evertonfc.com/evertontv** and register by entering a few simple details (don't forget to ask your mum or dad first!!).

Then, sit back, get comfy and enjoy hours upon hours of fantastic Toffees television!

The Official Everton App

The Club would be nothing without its supporters.

And supporting evertonfc.com is the Official Everton App!

Bringing you just as much news, all the very best exclusive interviews, video, audio and a whole lot more, it's the only way to put yourself one tap away from the best Everton updates.

To download the **Official Everton App** to your smartphone or tablet, search **'Everton'** in your app store. And don't worry, it's free!

Social Media

Everyone in the playground wants to be first in the know, don't they?

Super signing, a crucial piece of team news – whatever the big breaking scoop is coming out of Goodison Park, our official Twitter and Facebook feeds are the place to find out before anybody else!

And remember, nothing is confirmed until you read it on one of Everton's official pages!

To follow us on Twitter head to **twitter.com/Everton** or check out our Facebook page at **facebook.com/Everton.**

YouTube

Love watching clips of your favourite players, their best ever matches and most amazing goals?

Well, you'll love the official Everton YouTube page!

Like evertontv, our YouTube page is absolutely free but has even more tricks, flicks, fun and giggles!

As well as goals, look out for players going head-to-head at board games, having a crack at the crossbar challenge and also hilarious videos from the Everton outtakes archive!

Watch it all now at **youtube.com/officialeverton!**

GUESS THE WINNERS!

By the time you read your 2015 Official Everton Annual the footy season will be well under way. But there's still time to have a league of your own!

Here are some of the competitions that will be won and lost this season and all you need to do is write down who you think will win them. You will see that there is also space for two of your friends to join in.

You'll have a lot of fun following your predictions throughout the season and then when May comes around you can see who got the most right and win your own 2014/15 Prediction League!

Competition	You	Friend 1	Friend 2
Premier League			
Championship			
League One			
League Two			
FA Cup			
Capital One Cup			
Scottish Premier League			
Scottish Championship			
Scottish Cup			
Champions League			
Europa League			
Footballer of the Year			
Premier League Top Scorer			
Conference			
TOTAL			

LEON OSMAN

The summer of 2014 was a special one for LEON OSMAN as he celebrated his testimonial match. The Blues played Portuguese side FC Porto at Goodison Park on a warm August afternoon and almost 20,000 fans turned up to show their appreciation for his contribution over the years.

Since making his debut as a late substitute at Tottenham Hotspur in 2003 Ossie has played more than 300 Premier League games for Everton and at the end of last season he was closing in on 400 matches in all competitions.

Here are Ossie's life and times in pictures...

The Skelmersdale Junior League Footballer of the Year when he was 8

Leon is front row on the right in this Elmers Green FC team photo when he was 9 years old

After helping England Under-15s beat Germany

In action during the 1998 FA Youth Cup final against West Ham

Scoring the 2007/08 Everton Goal of the Season against Larissa at Goodison

Celebrating his first ever Goodison goal against West Brom in 2004

An England debut against Sweden in 2012

Smashing the ball into the net against Manchester City in 2013

Finding the net for the first time in a Merseyside derby in 2012

Challenging for the ball during the 2009 FA Cup final

STEVEN NAISMITH

ROBERTO MARTÍNEZ SAYS: *"He is enjoying his football, works extremely hard and he is one of the brightest footballing brains I have ever worked with. Steven is someone who can take information and execute it down to perfection and he has been a real strong character in the dressing room, bringing those strong attributes to the group."*

LEON OSMAN

SYLVAIN DISTIN SAYS: *"Leon is a great player and a funny guy as well. He is part of the reason why we have such a good atmosphere in the squad. He is always in a good mood and always working hard. He is a great guy and he really represents Everton – the Club is at this level because of guys like him. He is a very humble guy who is there for you if you need him. You need a guy like that in your team."*

BRYAN OVIEDO

LEIGHTON BAINES SAYS: *"Bryan has come into the side when needed and it's not an easy thing to do when you have been out of the team for a long time, so he deserves even more credit. He has put in top performances. It's harder to come into the team when you have been out of it for a long time, and that's a credit to his professionalism and the way he has looked after himself in between."*

STEVEN PIENAAR

LEIGHTON BAINES SAYS: *"I am made up to have him here. He makes a massive difference to us. When he trains, he changes training. That shows how good a player he is. Just his ability to take the ball in any situation; he never loses the ball and the worst case is he wins you a foul if he is struggling as he is such an intelligent player. We have got that understanding on the pitch, which came quite naturally, and it is a pleasure to play alongside him."*

JOEL ROBLES

ROBERTO MARTÍNEZ SAYS: *"I know what Joel can do as a young man. He is a keeper with terrific potential and is learning every day from Tim. That partnership fills me with confidence and I'm happy to share the responsibilities in whatever competition we have in front of us. When you get to know Joel he is such an impressive young man that nothing fazes him."*

JOHN STONES

SYLVAIN DISTIN SAYS: *"John's reading of the game is great and he has a good mentality. He's a big character and a great guy who is willing to listen and learn. I don't feel like you can teach anything to anyone unless they're willing to receive and he is. But to be honest he's learning really fast by himself and he doesn't need much advice."*

THE GREATEST EVER SEASON 30 YEARS ON!

OFFICIAL PROGRAMME 50p

Everton at GOODISON

EVERTON v
BAYERN MUNICH
European Cup Winners' Cup
Semi-final — 2nd Leg
Wednesday 24th April 1985

Inside Tonight's Programme...
PROFILE ON NEVILLE SOUTHALL
IN COLOUR – ACTION AND NEWS
FROM THE FIRST LEG IN MUNICH

After winning the FA Cup at Wembley in 1984, the Evertonians couldn't wait for the following season to start. Manager, Howard Kendall, had a talented squad of young players who had turned the club's fortunes around and were ready to bring the glory days back to Goodison Park.

Everton beat the League Champions Liverpool in the Charity Shield back at Wembley but the optimism was severely tested when Tottenham Hotspur came to Goodison on the opening day of the 1984/85 season and won 4-1.

The Toffees then lost at West Brom during the following week before finally getting off the mark with a Friday night 1-0 win at Chelsea's Stamford Bridge.

Everton were up and running and nothing was going to stop them.

The brilliant results flowed. A wonder-goal from Graeme Sharp earned a 1-0 win at Anfield and Manchester United were thrashed 5-0 at Goodison Park.

The wins just kept coming and before too long the supporters began to dream of a unique 'treble' as the team made

progress in the FA Cup and the European Cup Winners' Cup.

By April that treble was most definitely in Everton's sights.

Ipswich Town were beaten in the FA Cup quarter-final, following a replay, and in Europe an Andy Gray hat-trick paved the way for an aggregate victory over Dutch team Fortuna Sittard.

Both semi-finals were dramatic affairs.

In the FA Cup, Everton trailed to Luton Town at Villa Park and were on their way out of the competition until Kevin Sheedy scored a late free-kick to take the contest into extra-time. Luton had thought they'd done enough and they were deflated by Sheedy's strike

The first of them was the European Cup Winners' Cup in the Dutch city of Rotterdam against Rapid Vienna from Austria. The stadium was awash with supporters wearing the blue and white of Everton and the players didn't let them down.

The Toffees won 3-1, thanks to goals from Andy Gray, Trevor Steven and Kevin Sheedy.

Just four days later, the travelling Blue and White army descended on Wembley yet again for an FA Cup final against Manchester United. After a long and glorious season this was just one match too far and although United had a player (Kevin Moran) sent-off, they still won the Cup with an extra-time winner from Norman Whiteside.

Despite the disappointment, the Evertonians knew they'd seen the finest season in their team's history. Howard Kendall was the Manager of the Year, Neville Southall was the Footballer of the Year and Peter Reid was voted as the PFA Player of the Year.

so it was no real surprise when centre-half Derek Mountfield headed a winning goal for Everton.

In Europe, Kendall's men drew 0-0 in the semi-final first-leg away to Bayern Munich to set up a game that many still regard as Goodison Park's greatest ever night.

The stadium was packed to the rafters well before the kick-off and the atmosphere was electric as the two teams walked out for the kick-off. Some of the tackles and challenges from both sets of players were very aggressive and these days would probably have been punished by yellow or red cards!

To the dismay of the Evertonians, it was Bayern Munich who scored first through Dieter Hoeneß. That meant that Everton needed to score twice to progress through to the final. At half-time, Howard Kendall told his players to get the ball into the penalty area because 'the Gwladys Street will suck the ball into the net!'

The tactic worked. After a goalmouth scramble Graeme Sharp equalised and then Andy Gray put Everton ahead. Goodison was absolutely rocking and the roof nearly came off just before the end when Trevor Steven secured a 3-1 win.

In the old First Division, Everton were now unstoppable.

May 1985 was, quite simply, the greatest calendar month in the history of Everton Football Club!

The League title was wrapped up at Goodison Park thanks to a 2-0 win against Queens Park Rangers and left Everton with plenty of time to prepare for their two big finals.

WHERE ARE THEY NOW...?

NEVILLE SOUTHALL
Coaching youngsters in Wales

GARY STEVENS
A physiotherapist living in Australia

PAT van den HAUWE
Living in South Africa

KEVIN RATCLIFFE
A media pundit for BBC Wales

DEREK MOUNTFIELD
Coaching youngsters in Wirral

PETER REID
A media pundit after a long career in management

TREVOR STEVEN
A football agent living in Dubai

GRAEME SHARP
An Everton FC ambassador and media pundit with Radio City and Sky.

ANDY GRAY
A media pundit in Qatar

PAUL BRACEWELL
An Academy coach at Sunderland FC

KEVIN SHEEDY
Everton's Under-18s Academy coach.

TEN WITH MICHELLE!

We asked Everton Ladies captain MICHELLE HINNINGAN ten questions about her fab career in footy...

1 What do you love most about football?

I love the feeling of walking out onto the pitch every Sunday and knowing that your family are in the stands proudly watching. Football isn't just a game, it's my whole life and I have had to make huge sacrifices throughout my career. But I wouldn't change it for the world.

2 Can you remember the first time you kicked a ball and how you learned about the game?

I was about seven, watching my dad play football for the local team. My sister, cousins and I would be on the sidelines or back behind the goal playing shooties or headers and volleys for the whole 90 minutes!

3 Can you remember your first ever goal?

Yes it was in Everton Under-12s, with my head. The ball was crossed in and it would have been harder to miss to be honest. I just remember closing my eyes (now we've been taught not too!) and sticking my head on it.

4 How did you get involved in football?

My family are from a footballing background.

My uncle was a pro and my cousin was at the club when I first joined. But it was all down to my other cousin who would come down and play with me in the garden and then eventually let me go on the field and play with all his mates.

5 Did it benefit you playing with boys?

Yes, definitely. Boys will always be physically stronger and quicker than women at an older age but when I was playing with them as a kid, I was just as good as them, even better than most of them! I loved scoring goals against them or winning tackles – that made me enjoy playing with them even more. Playing with them gave me confidence and allowed me to go on and join Everton.

6 What is the best bit of advice you have been given?

From my parents – just go out and play with a smile and enjoy it. For me, I know if I am happy and enjoying it, then that's when I play at my best.

7 How did you join Everton?

I first joined Everton when I was 11. I had moved into senior school and had trials for the girls' football team. I got scouted for the school team on my second trial by an Everton scout whose daughter was playing at the time and he asked if I wanted to go down and train with them in Bootle. I haven't looked back. Must have been a good first session!

8 **Who were you friends with coming through?**

I have been friends with Toni Duggan since the age of 11 or 12. We both got our first call up to England at the same time. I turned up in my France tracksuit and I think she had the Argentina one on! We've been through the system together, from the Centre of Excellence through to the first team, so this year it was hard for me when she joined Man City as I was used to seeing her at training every night.

9 **Describe how it felt to make your first team debut?**

The feeling is unbelievable. I had been in and around the team for a couple of months and had made it to the bench. I remember Mo Marley telling me and

Toni to go and warm up. We were nervous and scared, and I think it was the quickest warm up we have ever done! We both just wanted to go on. That's a day I will never forget. The same season I was selected to go on tour with the first team to Canada – what an experience that was!

10 **How much do you enjoy playing for, and captaining, Everton?**

Words can't explain how much of an amazing club Everton is. I am lucky to have been a part of it from such a young age. From training, to games, and everything about the club – I love being a part of it. I know for a fact there is no other club like Everton. To then be captain is an amazing feeling. I couldn't have asked for a better group of girls and I know we will achieve great things together.

JAMES McCARTHY

Do you know how old James McCarthy was when he made his first team debut? Well done to all of you who said 15!

James was the same age as many of you reading this Annual. Imagine that – playing football against grown men! Scary right? It was a little bit for James as well. But through dedication and hard work, he not only held his own but became a really important player.

This was for Hamilton Academical, his first club up in Scotland. They were playing in the Scottish Championship, the second division up north, and manager Billy Reid had seen enough of the young midfielder in the youth team to see that he could do well in the first team.

So he threw him on against Queen of the South and James never looked back. So if you have dreamed of being a footballer then James McCarthy is great role model to follow.

Since that first game it's like someone has hit the fast forward button on his career – first team by 15, Premier League by 18, international football at 19. Crazy!

But all that has proved is that hard work pays off – and James knows all about hard work. He has constantly had to prove himself at every club he has been at, starting with showing he belonged in the Hamilton team at just 15.

"It was difficult," he recalls. "You were coming up against big men but to be honest, I never went into a game and looked at myself against an opponent and thought I was going to struggle. I just thought that I would give the best that I could give, and every week I did that. When I first broke in I scored against Livingston and became the club's youngest ever scorer."

James continued to progress and made the move to the Premier League with Wigan Athletic in 2009.

"Obviously the jump from the Scottish Premier League to the English Premier League is big and it was a big difference physically. I had to add a lot of stuff to my game and work hard. So that's what I did. In the end things worked out for me.

"During that early period at Wigan I was mentally strong because of what I had done previously at

Hamilton. I wanted to do it for myself. People were looking at me and saying to me during those first five or six months that I should have stayed at Hamilton because I wasn't good enough for the Premier League. But again, I had my family around me supporting me, wanting to push me on and off the pitch. Thankfully things started clicking for me and the gaffer gave me my chance and I took it."

That 'gaffer' was none other than Roberto Martínez!

James became a full Republic of Ireland international and won the FA Cup at Wembley whilst at Wigan before linking up with Roberto again at Everton.

"It has all gone fast!" he smiles. "A few people think I'm a bit older than I actually am because I have been about for a while. I'm 24 in November but getting on a bit in some people's eyes! I'm still learning each day. In training, I'm around some really experienced big name players and I take bits from them and just take each day as it comes."

So there you go, dreams do come true. But you have to work hard to achieve them!

SAMUEL ETO'O

In the summer of 2014, Samuel Eto'o became an Everton player.

The man who had previously played for Real Madrid, Barcelona, Inter Milan and Chelsea signed a two-year deal and was handed the number 5 jersey.

He brought with him a fantastic list of achievements and experience and his arrival at Goodison Park was greeted very enthusiastically by all Evertonians.

This is the story of one of Africa's greatest ever footballers...

He was born on 10 March 1981 in Douala, which is the largest city in Cameroon.

He made his international debut for Cameroon when he was just 15-years old.

Eto'o in his Chelsea Strip

When he was 16-years old he left Cameroon to join Real Madrid's Academy.

He represented Cameroon at the 1998 World Cup when he was 17.

After failing to become a Madrid regular he joined Real Mallorca in 2000.

By the time he left Mallorca in 2004 to join Barcelona, he was their all-time leading Spanish League (La Liga) goalscorer.

With Barcelona, Eto'o won three La Liga titles and one Copa del Rey (Spanish Cup).

He also won the Champions League twice with Barca (beating Arsenal in the final in 2006 and Manchester United in 2009).

Samuel Eto'o at Inter Milan

He holds the record for the number of appearances by an African player in the La Liga.

In 2009 he left Barcelona and signed for Inter Milan.

In 2009 Eto'o had won the Champions League, the Spanish League and the Spanish Cup. In 2010, with Inter Milan, he won the Champions League again, the Italian League and the Italian Cup! He is the only man to ever win two 'trebles' in consecutive seasons.

In 2011 he moved to Russia to join Anzhi Makhachkala.

He moved to the Premier League in 2013 when he signed for Chelsea.

Eto'o posing with his Everton strip

He has won the African Footballer of the Year a record four times (in 2003, 2004, 2005 and 2010).

He is Cameroon's all-time leading goalscorer.

He is the all-time leading goalscorer in the African Cup of Nations.

In August 2014 Samuel Eto'o signed for Everton!

Eto'o playing for his home nation

NAME THE MASCOT

The Everton mascot, Changy the Elephant, is a familiar sight around Goodison Park on a matchday. Changy mingles with supporters in and around the Fan Zone, posing for photographs and leading the singing and dancing!

Changy is, of course, named after our main sponsors who use the elephant logo on their products. But did you know that in Thailand the elephant is a symbol of strength, wisdom and harmony?

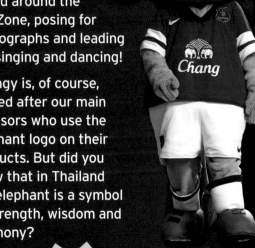

At Goodison Park on a matchday, Everton in the Community's Megan Griffiths is the human body inside the Changy suit.

"It's great for me because I love mixing with the fans," she said. "The young children love meeting Changy and I have lost count of the number of photographs I have posed for with the kids! The Chang costume comes in separate parts but after a bit of practice I can get it on in about five minutes. The reception that Changy gets from our fans is brilliant and although I am biased I think we've got the best mascot in the Premier League."

Have a look at these photographs of other mascots from around the country and see how many you can recognise...

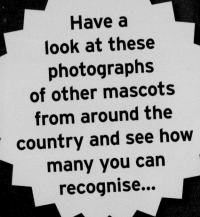

1

2

3

4

5

Answers on page 60-61.

LEIGHTON BAINES

Ever wondered what Leighton Baines's favourite band was? If you are a Baines fanatic, you'll know that our left back is big into his music.

He loves his music that much that he's even mates with a few musicians – one of his best pals is Miles Kane!

He also knows the lads from the Arctic Monkeys and has been backstage at big festivals like Glastonbury and T in the Park.

So we decided to have a chat to the England international about his favourite tunes...

Hi Leighton! What music do you like listening to?

LB: My musical tastes are just generally whatever my ear likes! I would say it is predominantly guitar based, but I'm still trying to broaden my horizons by listening to different stuff when I can. So whatever stuff you like that you think I may be interested in, please let me know, and I will give it a listen. I'll warn you now through – things like modern versions of R'n'B are just not my cup of tea!

Who are your favourite artists?

LB: Bob Dylan is basically the greatest lyricist ever. Pink Floyd are the most innovative band of all time – they pushed boundaries with their music, lyrics and live shows. Then you have The Beatles who are easily the most influential band that has existed. The Arctic Monkeys are an amazing band that I feel like I have grown up with and they have always been in keeping with how my tastes have developed... lucky me! Paul Weller is a fantastic musician who has influenced a lot of British bands over the years.

How did you get into music?

LB: Growing up, my parents would have tapes on in the car like Phil Collins, REM, Deacon Blue and that sort of stuff. As an early teenager I remember I started to get into Oasis, Travis, Cast, Space etc. But a few years later I got into all sorts. I remember I even used to go into my sister's room and listen to her Spice Girls album!! Then I got into hip-hop – 50 Cent and all that!

I got into Dizzy Rascal's first album, so started to listen to stuff along that UK garage vibe. Like I said, I think I just follow whatever my ear likes! Obviously, as I have grown up I look back at some of the stuff I used to like and cringe but that's all part of the process!

As a footballer, is it hard to get to gigs?

LB: Yeah, it can be. Obviously my main priority has to be football and when we have a game I tend to do very little in the 48 hours before. That means that on a typical week when we play on a Saturday, Thursday and Friday for me are generally about training and starting to prepare for the game which means getting the right amount of rest. So, as you can imagine, when we play a midweek game too it pretty much writes off the whole week!

You also play the guitar don't you?

LB: Yeah. I take my guitar away with me when I travel with England and have a practice. I think music is a little thing to escape into. Once I come away from training I

can't be bothered watching football on the TV and the news, but I love playing my guitar and I wouldn't swap it for anything.

You've got a few famous music mates as well haven't you?

LB: I've met Alex Turner from the Arctic Monkeys but that was a bit mad because he's a total hero! I have also known Miles Kane a while. I'd been a big fan of what Miles has done for ages. I was at a WWE wrestling match with my son and we bumped into him. I wasn't sure whether he knew who I was, but we got chatting and swapped numbers.

He lived above this coffee-shop and I started going over spend time with him talking music in his flat. We've become good mates ever since.

What do the rest of the lads in the Everton dressing room like?

LB: There's a playlist mix that the lads at Everton listen to in the changing-room before and after a game. The lads mostly chose hip-hop and R&B, but I've tried to open their eyes and introduce some other stuff, which doesn't always go down well. But since I've been playing Miles's stuff to them, someone has taken it upon themselves to add some of his singles – "Come Closer" and "Inhaler" – to the mix. It's only one in every 15, but it's nice to hear it pop up!

THE SONGKRAN WATER FESTIVAL

The Songkran Festival is celebrated in Thailand every April to mark the start of the Thai New Year and, as our great friends and main sponsor Chang are from that country, Everton always joins in.

The traditional way to celebrate is for the people to have a lot of fun throwing water around, which is meant as a symbol of washing all of the bad away and is sometimes filled with fragrant herbs.

At Everton, the water festival was celebrated by John Stones, Steven Naismith and James McCarthy who jumped into the Finch Farm swimming pool, in the training kit, armed with water guns!

As you can see, they had a great time...!

NAME THE BOSS...

How well do you know the men who sit in the opposite dug-out to Roberto on a match-day? Here are eight Premier League managers when they were a bit younger (and in some cases a bit thinner!).

They are the bosses when they were players!

See how many you can name...

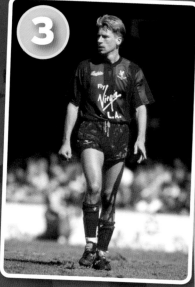

Answers on page 60-61.

GROWN UP QUIZ

Here's a page that you can show the grown-ups!

**Let them try this quiz and see if they score as
many points as you did on the Junior Quiz page 35**

1. For which team did Gareth Barry make his professional debut?

2. From which Russian team did Everton sign Aiden McGeady?

3. Who did Everton play in the 3rd round of the FA Cup last season?

4. When Roberto Martínez and his assistant Graeme Jones once played on opposing teams in a Scottish Premier League match, what two teams were they playing for?

5. At which stadium did Everton play Celta Vigo in August 2014?

6. Which three club sides, other than Everton, did Duncan Ferguson play for during his career?

7. From which team did the Blues sign Muhamed Bešić?

8. Who was the last ex-Everton player to win a World Cup winners medal?

9. Who scored Everton's last FA Cup goal of last season?

10. Who did the Toffees beat 2-0 on the last day of last season?

11. And which former Everton player played for the opposition that day?

12. And who made his Everton Premier League debut on the same day?

13. At the start of this current season which two former Everton players were managing in the Premier League?

14. Which four teams has Sylvain Distin play for in the Premier League?

15. From which team did Everton sign Seamus Coleman?

Answers on page 60-61.

QUIZ ANSWERS

Page 16 & 17
INTERNATIONAL BLUES

Lee Carsley – Ireland

Nuno Valente – Portugal

Louis Saha – France

Thomas Gravesen – Denmark

Tim Cahill – Australia

Landon Donovan – USA

Segundo Castillo – Ecuador

Joseph Yobo – Nigeria

Diniyar Bilyaletdinov – Russia

John Heitinga – Holland

Page 20
WORDSEARCH

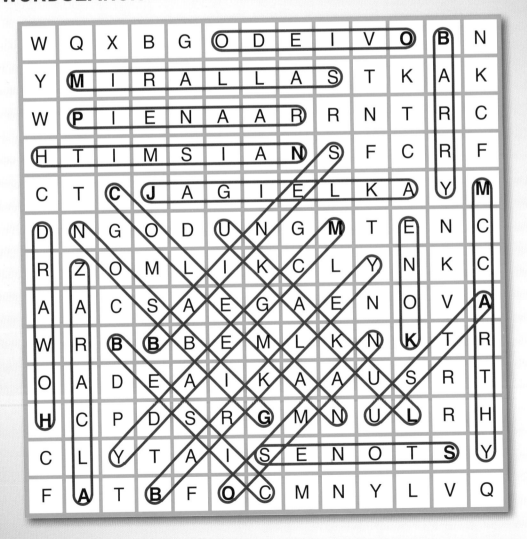

Page 32
WHO DID I PLAY FOR?

1) Ivory Coast
2) Spain
3) Bosnia Herzegovina
4) Argentina
5) Ecuador
6) Mexico
7) Holland
8) Uruguay
9) USA
10) Brazil

Page 33
WORLD CUP QUIZ

1) Germany won 7-1
2) Daniel Sturridge and Wayne Rooney
3) Joseph Yobo
4) James Rodríguez
5) Oscar, David Luiz, Willian, Ramires
6) 5-1
7) None
8) Three
9) 21
10) Russia

Page 35
JUNIOR QUIZ

1) Paraguay
2) John Heitinga
3) Swansea City
4) Fulham
5) Kejian
6) Sheffield United
7) Bullens Road
8) Nikica Jelavić v Liverpool 2012
9) Sheffield Wednesday and Leeds United
10) Hull City and we won 2-0
11) Romelu Lukaku got two
    and Kevin Mirallas
12) Ross Barkley, Romelu Lukaku
    and Leon Osman
13) John Stones
14) Italy, Uruguay and Costa Rica;
15) Heitinga

Page 52 & 53
NAME THE MASCOT

1) Chelsea
2) Crystal Palace
3) West Ham
4) Leicester City
5) Hull City
6) Tottenham Hotspur
7) Manchester City
8) Arsenal
9) QPR
10) Sunderland
11) Manchester United
12) West Brom
13) Burnley
14) Stoke City

Page 58
NAME THE BOSS

1) Mark Hughes
2) Steve Bruce
3) Alan Pardew
4) Tony Pulis
5) Sam Allardyce
6) Paul Lambert
7) Gus Poyet
8) Harry Redknapp

Page 59
GROWN UP QUIZ

1) Aston Villa
2) Spartak Moscow
3) QPR
4) Roberto was at Motherwell, Graeme
   was at St Johnstone
5) Prenton Park, Tranmere Rovers
6) Dundee United, Rangers and Newcastle
7) Ferencváros
8) Shkodran Mustafi for Germany in 2014
9) Romelu Lukaku
10) Hull City
11) Nikica Jelavić
12) Lacina Traoré
13) Mark Hughes and Alan Irvine
14) Newcastle, Manchester City,
    Portsmouth and Everton
15) Sligo Rovers